Gothic Poems of Love, Life, and Loss

By

Various

Read &' Co.

Published by Ragged Hand,
an imprint of Read & Co.

This edition published by Read & Co. in 2023

Extra material © 2023 Read & Co. Books

A catalogue record for this book is available
from the British Library.

ISBN: 9781528722896

Read & Co. is part of Read Books Ltd.
For more information visit www.readandcobooks.co.uk

It may not be generally known, that Gothic poetry, is much like that style of architecture, wonderfully enriched all over with images and tracery.

—*The Literary Life of Miscellanies of John Galt*, 1834

Contents

An Excerpt

By Richard Garnett

But much that is noble and heroic in the feelings of the nineteenth century has its hidden roots in the thirteenth. Gothic architecture and Gothic poetry are the children of the same mother; and if the true but unadorned language of the heart, the aspirations of a real faith, the sorrow and joy of a true love, are still listened to by the nations of Europe; and if what is called the Romantic school is strong enough to hold its ground against the classical taste and its royal patrons, such as Louis XIV., Charles II., and Frederick the Great, we owe it to those chivalrous poets who dared for the first time to be what they were, and to say what they felt, and to whom Faith, Love, and Honor were worthy subjects of poetry...

An excerpt from
The Universal Anthology..., 1890

Gothic Poetry

An Excerpt

… Let me linger for a moment upon this interesting subject. 'To appreciate the charms whether of classic or Gothic poetry, the reader must possess the inward eye of taste. That clear and serene organ of intellectual vision which looks not only into all the component elements of the object before it, but gazes even beyond the visible into the invisible, and perceives not only the beauty and splendour of the actual creation, but also the remote array of thoughts and images which, being present to the creative transports of the poet, are, as it were, thrown into shadow, and intercepted by a veil from the eyes of the vulgar. Let me illustrate this remark from the sister art of painting.

When Paul Veronese was asked why certain figures were painted in shade, no cause of shadow being apparent in the picture itself, he immediately answered, "A cloud is passing the sky, which has overshadowed them." The reader of Homer, or Milton, or Shakspeare, or Dante, might expect to receive a similar reply. No delineation by the pen of genius can be properly admired or understood, without the perspective, and retrospective, and circumspective eyesight of the mind. Imagination, transparent as it is with its own internal and glorious light, can, nevertheless, turn a dark side to the weak vision of unilluminated common sense, or the enfeebled and diseased eyesight of a licentious fancy. To the first, the Faérie Queene would only be a series of dull pictures by a dull painter; to the second, Paradise Lost would only be, as it was to Waller, a poem written by a blind old schoolmaster, and remarkable for nothing but its extreme length ...

An excerpt from
Fraser's Magazine, Volume 27, 1843

The Romantic Feeling

An Excerpt by Montague Summers

Literature in every age presents itself under one of two forms, neither of which can ever be arbitrary or accidental, since both, however separate in their tendencies and aims have their roots deep down in man's philosophical or religious speculation. In the one case literature expresses and discusses under various shapes, as elegantly and masterly as its exponents are able, the prevailing ideas concerning the problems, material and metaphysical, of the current hour. It is a clear reflection, and brightly burnished is the mirror, of everyday life. The common man, to take a phrase from Dr. Johnson, "feels what he remembers to have felt before, but he feels it with a great increase of sensibility." He is pleased because he finds the fleet yet haunting thoughts he was seeking to disentangle and digest in his own mind are set out before him in order, far better than he himself could have arranged his ideas. The answers to the problems and the conclusions may not be such as he approves or would accept, but no matter, the inquiry has been made, and even by his mere regard, his reading the pages quite cursorily, he feels that he has in some sort taken his individual part and had a main share in the argument.

On the other hand literature may lead a man away from life, as it were, that is to say it may direct him from the long and often fruitless contemplation of the circumstances which surround him, his journey-work, to many distasteful, monotonous to most, and invite his attention to other realities and aspirations, flinging wide

Magic casements, opening on the foam
Of perilous seas, in faery lands forlorn.

This is the essence of the romantic spirit. Romanticism weans our thought and care from the sordid practicalities of the repeated round; it offers us a wider and fuller vision; and it is therefore subjective; it is reactionary in its revolt against the present since it yearns for the loveliness of the past as so picturesquely revealed to us in art and poem; and informed by a passionate desire for the beautiful, which can never be entirely satisfied but is always craving for more, it must by its very nature remain always unappeased, that is to say in some sense dimly seeking adventure in the realms of the mind, intellectually restless and aspiring.

An excerpt from
The Gothic Quest, 1938

Eternal Obsessions

Sir Walter Raleigh
(1552–1618)

A Farewell to False Love

Farewell, false love, the oracle of lies,
A mortal foe and enemy to rest,
An envious boy, from whom all cares arise,
A bastard vile, a beast with rage possessed,
A way of error, a temple full of treason,
In all effects contrary unto reason.

A poisoned serpent covered all with flowers,
Mother of sighs, and murderer of repose,
A sea of sorrows whence are drawn such showers
As moisture lend to every grief that grows;
A school of guile, a net of deep deceit,
A gilded hook that holds a poisoned bait.

A fortress foiled, which reason did defend,
A siren song, a fever of the mind,
A maze wherein affection finds no end,
A raging cloud that runs before the wind,
A substance like the shadow of the sun,
A goal of grief for which the wisest run.

A quenchless fire, a nurse of trembling fear,
A path that leads to peril and mishap,
A true retreat of sorrow and despair,
An idle boy that sleeps in pleasure's lap,
A deep mistrust of that which certain seems,
A hope of that which reason doubtful deems.

Sith then thy trains my younger years betrayed,
And for my faith ingratitude I find;
And sith repentance hath my wrongs bewrayed,
Whose course was ever contrary to kind:
False love, desire, and beauty frail, adieu!
Dead is the root whence all these fancies grew.

William Shakespeare
(1564–1616)

Sonnet 3

Look in thy glass and tell the face thou viewest,
Now is the time that face should form another,
Whose fresh repair if now thou not renewest,
Thou dost beguile the world, unbless some mother.
For where is she so fair whose uneared womb
Disdains the tillage of thy husbandry?
Or who is he so fond will be the tomb
Of his self-love, to stop posterity?
Thou art thy mother's glass, and she in thee
Calls back the lovely April of her prime;
So thou through windows of thine age shalt see,
Despite of wrinkles, this thy golden time.
    But if thou live rememb'red not to be,
      Die single, and thine image dies with thee.

Sonnet 4

Unthrifty loveliness, why dost thou spend
Upon thy self thy beauty's legacy?
Nature's bequest gives nothing, but doth lend,
And being frank she lends to those are free:
Then, beauteous niggard, why dost thou abuse
The bounteous largess given thee to give?
Profitless usurer, why dost thou use
So great a sum of sums, yet canst not live?
For having traffic with thy self alone,
Thou of thy self thy sweet self dost deceive:
Then how when nature calls thee to be gone,
What acceptable audit canst thou leave?
 Thy unused beauty must be tombed with thee,
 Which, used, lives th' executor to be.

William Blake
(1757–1827)

The Sick Rose

O Rose thou art sick.
The invisible worm,
That flies in the night
In the howling storm:

Has found out thy bed
Of crimson joy:
And his dark secret love
Does thy life destroy.

Anne Bannerman
(1765–1829)

The Mermaid

"When, at last, they retired to rest, Ajut went down to the
beach, where finding a fishing-boat, she entered it without
hesitation, and, telling those, who wondered at her
rashness, that she was going in search of Anningait, rowed
away, with great swiftness, and was seen no more.

The fate of those lovers gave occasion to various fictions and
conjectures. Some are of opinion, that they were changed
into stars; others imagine, Anningait was seized, in his
passage, by the Genius of the Rocks, and that Ajut was
transformed into a Mermaid, and still continues to seek
her lover, in the deserts of the sea." —RAMBLER, No. 187.

Blow on, ye death-fraught whirlwinds! blow,
    Around the rocks, and rifted caves;
  Ye demons of the gulf below!
    I hear you, in the troubled waves.
  High on this cliff, which darkness shrouds
  In night's impenetrable clouds,
  My solitary watch I keep,
  And listen, while the turbid deep
Groans to the raging tempests, as they roll
Their desolating force, to thunder at the pole.

  Eternal world of waters, hail!
    Within thy caves my Lover lies;
  And day and night alike shall fail,
    Ere slumber lock my streaming eyes.
  Along this wild untrodden coast,
  Heap'd by the gelid hand of frost;
  Thro' this unbounded waste of seas,
  Where never sigh'd the vernal breeze;
Mine was the choice, in this terrific form,
To brave the icy surge, to shiver in the storm.

Yes! I am chang'd.—My heart, my soul,
    Retain no more their former glow.
Hence, ere the black'ning tempests roll,
    I watch the bark, in murmurs low,
(While darker low'rs the thick'ning gloom)
To lure the sailor to his doom;
Soft from some pile of frozen snow
I pour the syren-song of woe;
Like the sad mariner's expiring cry,
As, faint and worn with toil, he lays him down to die.

Then, while the dark and angry deep
    Hangs his huge billows high in air;
And the wild wind with awful sweep,
    Howls in each fitful swell—beware!
Firm on the rent and crashing mast,
I lend new fury to the blast;
I mark each hardy cheek grow pale,
And the proud sons of courage fail;
Till the torn vessel drinks the surging waves,
Yawns the disparted main, and opes its shelving graves.

When Vengeance bears along the wave
    The spell, which heav'n and earth appals;
Alone, by night, in darksome cave,
    On me the gifted wizard calls.
Above the ocean's boiling flood
Thro' vapour glares the moon in blood:
Low sounds along the waters die,
And shrieks of anguish fill the sky;
Convulsive powers the solid rocks divide,
While, o'er the heaving surge, the embodied spirits glide.

Thrice welcome to my weary sight,
    Avenging ministers of wrath!
Ye heard, amid the realms of night,
    The spell that wakes the sleep of death.
Where Hecla's flames the snows dissolve,
Or storms, the polar skies involve;
Where, o'er the tempest-beaten wreck,
The raging winds and billows break;
On the sad earth, and in the stormy sea,
All, all shall shudd'ring own your potent agency.

To aid your toils, to scatter death,
    Swift, as the sheeted lightning's force,
When the keen north-wind's freezing breath
    Spreads desolation in its course,
My soul within this icy sea,
Fulfils her fearful destiny.
Thro' Time's long ages I shall wait
To lead the victims to their fate;
With callous heart, to hidden rocks decoy,
And lure, in seraph-strains, unpitying, to destroy.

Basil

THE sobbings of the ocean waves
Were all the notes that Basil knew;
He lov'd them since his ear could dwell
With gladness on their first low swell,
When the soft south-wind blew:

Like a wild flow'r of the wilderness,
He grew, amid the mountain air;
The rock had been his cradle-bed,
And never were his slumbers made
The holier for a mother's pray'r!

The skies, the woods, the winding shore,
Were imag'd on his desert breast;
His deep, dark eye was stern and keen,
It was the fire of soul unseen,
Unknown, untutor'd, unrepress'd . . .

The rude sea-boy was all the name
That every tongue to Basil gave;
The rude sea wind had marr'd his face,
But his heart! . . . 'twas Pity's resting place.
And he sung dirges for the dead,
In music like the mournful wave:

Young Basil wrought the fisher's nets,
And plied the heavy oar;
A lonely home he had! but oh!
That aught, that bore the human form,
Should bear the night, and nightly storm,
In that hut, on the wild sea-shore!

Yet there were hearts that beat and heav'd,
With flutt'ring love and tender joy,
To hear th' unprison'd tempest rise,
When all were safe from wind and skies,
And winter's keen inclemency!

But there was none whose eye pursu'd
This youth's unfollow'd footsteps home;
And he had steel'd his heart to bear,
Till the pulse, that should have quiver'd there,
Was feelingless and numb! . . .

The tones, that sooth'd this lonely heart
Came not from human kind!
He watch'd the breeze that sigh'd along,
To him it was the even-song
Of some hallow'd seraph-mind;

And then the sun would leave behind
Such lovely tints on cloud and tree;
O, how unlike this jarring world
That silentness of place and hour!
As if a breath would overpow'r
The murmur of the sea:

And from the stars of Heaven he drew
His picture of a place of rest!
Their sacred light was so serene,
It settled on his soul like love,
When he number'd every orb above
As the brothers of his breast . . .

But one drear night the stars withdrew
As Basil reach'd his shed;
The drifting torrent rattled rude
On the creaking rafts of shatter'd wood,
That stretch'd above his head.

Basil had heard the mountain storm
And the winter tempest beat;
Night after night he had slept, when shut,
Alone, within that rocking hut,
With the snow-wreaths at his feet;

But the awe, the dread that o'er him came,
This fateful night he quak'd to feel!
It was not fear of tide or wind, . . .
'Twas that low breathlessness of mind,
When the heart-veins congeal.

Whether it was the billow's sob,
Or the wild sea-eagle's cry,
He heard a moan that seem'd to come
From some lost wretch, that made his home
Of the desert and the sky!

It nearer came, till it sunk at once
Close to his unfasten'd door, . . .
The stifled groan was a voice in death,
And he could count the ebbing breath,
Till his own would note no more!

Then he heard footsteps rattling run
Across the frozen hill;
Their least, last sound, his stunned ear
Would measure, as if coming near,
They rung around him still!

But the weight that fell without, the corse,
As he had heard it die,
Thro' the spaces of his window-bars,
By the dawn-light he just could trace,
Where it lay along upon its face,
As life did never lie! . . .

Poor Basil wrench'd the feeble bar
To leave that dreary shed,
'Twas all too narrow for his flight,
And it robb'd his starting eyes of sight,
That he must cross the dead . . .

With frantic arm he burst the door,
That shiver'd to to his blow;
One step, . . . but oh! that one to take,
He wish'd that life had been the stake,
That he might have giv'n it now:

And on that long, dread night, he thought,
Till it settled on his brain;
And his heart grew bold,...for, at break of morn,
He had reach'd a rock, where a cave was worn
By the surges of the main . . .

The hours went on till fall of eve,
And the stars arose again!
Basil must make the rock his bed,
For his mountain-home is tenanted
By the spirit of the slain . . .

He wanders on the desert beach,
Like some lone ghost of air,
Scarce human like, . . . but then, his eye
Retains the keen and fiery dye
That wont to kindle there!

His dreams! the hopes that o'er his soul
Had wander'd of a brighter scene !
They sometimes come to soothe him still,
Such as he imag'd them at even,
When his joy was in the light of Heaven,
Where all was so serene.

But wilder fits and drearier dreams
Will oft upon him come;
And, when his brain is most perturb'd,
He drags his worn and naked feet
Across the crag, whose chasms meet,
To gaze on his forsaken home! . . .

The harsh sea-birds inhabit it
With the spirit of the slain!
And close beside, a heap of stones,
Is laid above these hollow bones,
That the mariner can see afar,
As a beacon, on the main.

Samuel Taylor Coleridge
(1772–1834)

Kubla Khan

Or, a vision in a dream. A Fragment.

In Xanadu did Kubla Khan
A stately pleasure-dome decree:
Where Alph, the sacred river, ran
Through caverns measureless to man
   Down to a sunless sea.
So twice five miles of fertile ground
With walls and towers were girdled round;
And there were gardens bright with sinuous rills,
Where blossomed many an incense-bearing tree;
And here were forests ancient as the hills,
Enfolding sunny spots of greenery.

But oh! that deep romantic chasm which slanted
Down the green hill athwart a cedarn cover!
A savage place! as holy and enchanted
As e'er beneath a waning moon was haunted
By woman wailing for her demon-lover!
And from this chasm, with ceaseless turmoil
   seething,
As if this earth in fast thick pants were breathing,
A mighty fountain momently was forced:
Amid whose swift half-intermitted burst
Huge fragments vaulted like rebounding hail,
Or chaffy grain beneath the thresher's flail:
And mid these dancing rocks at once and ever
It flung up momently the sacred river.
Five miles meandering with a mazy motion
Through wood and dale the sacred river ran,
Then reached the caverns measureless to man,
And sank in tumult to a lifeless ocean;
And 'mid this tumult Kubla heard from far
Ancestral voices prophesying war!
   The shadow of the dome of pleasure
    Floated midway on the waves;
   Where was heard the mingled measure
    From the fountain and the caves.

It was a miracle of rare device,
A sunny pleasure-dome with caves of ice!

A damsel with a dulcimer
In a vision once I saw:
It was an Abyssinian maid
And on her dulcimer she played,
Singing of Mount Abora.
Could I revive within me
Her symphony and song,
To such a deep delight 'twould win me,
That with music loud and long,
I would build that dome in air,
That sunny dome! those caves of ice!
And all who heard should see them there,
And all should cry, Beware! Beware!
His flashing eyes, his floating hair!
Weave a circle round him thrice,
And close your eyes with holy dread
For he on honey-dew hath fed,
And drunk the milk of Paradise.

Christabel

Part I

'Tis the middle of night by the castle clock,
And the owls have awakened the crowing cock;
Tu—whit! Tu—whoo!
And hark, again! the crowing cock,
How drowsily it crew.
Sir Leoline, the Baron rich,
Hath a toothless mastiff bitch;
From her kennel beneath the rock
She maketh answer to the clock,
Four for the quarters, and twelve for the hour;
Ever and aye, by shine and shower,
Sixteen short howls, not over loud;
Some say, she sees my lady's shroud.

Is the night chilly and dark?
The night is chilly, but not dark.
The thin gray cloud is spread on high,
It covers but not hides the sky.
The moon is behind, and at the full;

And yet she looks both small and dull.
The night is chill, the cloud is gray:
'Tis a month before the month of May,
And the Spring comes slowly up this way.

The lovely lady, Christabel,
Whom her father loves so well,
What makes her in the wood so late,
A furlong from the castle gate?
She had dreams all yesternight
Of her own betrothèd knight;
And she in the midnight wood will pray
For the weal of her lover that's far away.

She stole along, she nothing spoke,
The sighs she heaved were soft and low,
And naught was green upon the oak
But moss and rarest misletoe:
She kneels beneath the huge oak tree,
And in silence prayeth she.

The lady sprang up suddenly,
The lovely lady Christabel!
It moaned as near, as near can be,

But what it is she cannot tell.—
On the other side it seems to be,
Of the huge, broad-breasted, old oak tree.

The night is chill; the forest bare;
Is it the wind that moaneth bleak?
There is not wind enough in the air
To move away the ringlet curl
From the lovely lady's cheek—
There is not wind enough to twirl
The one red leaf, the last of its clan,
That dances as often as dance it can,
Hanging so light, and hanging so high,
On the topmost twig that looks up at the sky.

Hush, beating heart of Christabel!
Jesu, Maria, shield her well!
She folded her arms beneath her cloak,
And stole to the other side of the oak.
      What sees she there?

There she sees a damsel bright,
Drest in a silken robe of white,
That shadowy in the moonlight shone:

The neck that made that white robe wan,
Her stately neck, and arms were bare;
Her blue-veined feet unsandl'd were,
And wildly glittered here and there
The gems entangled in her hair.
I guess, 'twas frightful there to see
A lady so richly clad as she—
Beautiful exceedingly!

Mary mother, save me now!
(Said Christabel) And who art thou?

The lady strange made answer meet,
And her voice was faint and sweet:—
Have pity on my sore distress,
I scarce can speak for weariness:
Stretch forth thy hand, and have no fear!
Said Christabel, How camest thou here?
And the lady, whose voice was faint and sweet,
Did thus pursue her answer meet:—

My sire is of a noble line,
And my name is Geraldine:
Five warriors seized me yestermorn,

Me, even me, a maid forlorn:
They choked my cries with force and fright,
And tied me on a palfrey white.
The palfrey was as fleet as wind,
And they rode furiously behind.
They spurred amain, their steeds were white:
And once we crossed the shade of night.
As sure as Heaven shall rescue me,
I have no thought what men they be;
Nor do I know how long it is
(For I have lain entranced I wis)
Since one, the tallest of the five,
Took me from the palfrey's back,
A weary woman, scarce alive.
Some muttered words his comrades spoke:
He placed me underneath this oak;
He swore they would return with haste;
Whither they went I cannot tell—
I thought I heard, some minutes past,
Sounds as of a castle bell.
Stretch forth thy hand (thus ended she).
And help a wretched maid to flee.

Then Christabel stretched forth her hand,
And comforted fair Geraldine:
O well, bright dame! may you command
The service of Sir Leoline;
And gladly our stout chivalry
Will he send forth and friends withal
To guide and guard you safe and free
Home to your noble father's hall.

She rose: and forth with steps they passed
That strove to be, and were not, fast.
Her gracious stars the lady blest,
And thus spake on sweet Christabel:
All our household are at rest,
The hall as silent as the cell;
Sir Leoline is weak in health,
And may not well awakened be,
But we will move as if in stealth,
And I beseech your courtesy,
This night, to share your couch with me.

They crossed the moat, and Christabel
Took the key that fitted well;
A little door she opened straight,

All in the middle of the gate;
The gate that was ironed within and without,
Where an army in battle array had marched out.
The lady sank, belike through pain,
And Christabel with might and main
Lifted her up, a weary weight,
Over the threshold of the gate:
Then the lady rose again,
And moved, as she were not in pain.

So free from danger, free from fear,
They crossed the court: right glad they were.
And Christabel devoutly cried
To the lady by her side,
Praise we the Virgin all divine
Who hath rescued thee from thy distress!
Alas, alas! said Geraldine,
I cannot speak for weariness.
So free from danger, free from fear,
They crossed the court: right glad they were.

Outside her kennel, the mastiff old
Lay fast asleep, in moonshine cold.
The mastiff old did not awake,

Yet she an angry moan did make!
And what can ail the mastiff bitch?
Never till now she uttered yell
Beneath the eye of Christabel.
Perhaps it is the owlet's scritch:
For what can ail the mastiff bitch?

They passed the hall, that echoes still,
Pass as lightly as you will!
The brands were flat, the brands were dying,
Amid their own white ashes lying;
But when the lady passed, there came
A tongue of light, a fit of flame;
And Christabel saw the lady's eye,
And nothing else saw she thereby,
Save the boss of the shield of Sir Leoline tall,
Which hung in a murky old niche in the wall.
O softly tread, said Christabel,
My father seldom sleepeth well.

Sweet Christabel her feet doth bare,
And jealous of the listening air
They steal their way from stair to stair,
Now in glimmer, and now in gloom,

And now they pass the Baron's room,
As still as death, with stifled breath!
And now have reached her chamber door;
And now doth Geraldine press down
The rushes of the chamber floor.

The moon shines dim in the open air,
And not a moonbeam enters here.
But they without its light can see
The chamber carved so curiously,
Carved with figures strange and sweet,
All made out of the carver's brain,
For a lady's chamber meet:
The lamp with twofold silver chain
Is fastened to an angel's feet.

The silver lamp burns dead and dim;
But Christabel the lamp will trim.
She trimmed the lamp, and made it bright,
And left it swinging to and fro,
While Geraldine, in wretched plight,
Sank down upon the floor below.

O weary lady, Geraldine,
I pray you, drink this cordial wine!
It is a wine of virtuous powers;
My mother made it of wild flowers.

And will your mother pity me,
Who am a maiden most forlorn?
Christabel answered—Woe is me!
She died the hour that I was born.
I have heard the grey-haired friar tell
How on her death-bed she did say,
That she should hear the castle-bell
Strike twelve upon my wedding-day.
O mother dear! that thou wert here!
I would, said Geraldine, she were!

But soon with altered voice, said she—
'Off, wandering mother! Peak and pine!
I have power to bid thee flee.'
Alas! what ails poor Geraldine?
Why stares she with unsettled eye?
Can she the bodiless dead espy?

And why with hollow voice cries she,
'Off, woman, off! this hour is mine—
Though thou her guardian spirit be,
Off, woman, off! 'tis given to me.'

Then Christabel knelt by the lady's side,
And raised to heaven her eyes so blue—
Alas! said she, this ghastly ride—
Dear lady! it hath wildered you!
The lady wiped her moist cold brow,
And faintly said, ' 'tis over now!'

Again the wild-flower wine she drank:
Her fair large eyes 'gan glitter bright,
And from the floor whereon she sank,
The lofty lady stood upright:
She was most beautiful to see,
Like a lady of a far countrèe.

And thus the lofty lady spake—
'All they who live in the upper sky,
Do love you, holy Christabel!
And you love them, and for their sake
And for the good which me befel,

Even I in my degree will try,
Fair maiden, to requite you well.
But now unrobe yourself; for I
Must pray, ere yet in bed I lie.'

Quoth Christabel, So let it be!
And as the lady bade, did she.
Her gentle limbs did she undress,
And lay down in her loveliness.

But through her brain of weal and woe
So many thoughts moved to and fro,
That vain it were her lids to close;
So half-way from the bed she rose,
And on her elbow did recline
To look at the lady Geraldine.

Beneath the lamp the lady bowed,
And slowly rolled her eyes around;
Then drawing in her breath aloud,
Like one that shuddered, she unbound
The cincture from beneath her breast:
Her silken robe, and inner vest,
Dropt to her feet, and full in view,

Behold! her bosom and half her side—
A sight to dream of, not to tell!
O shield her! shield sweet Christabel!

Yet Geraldine nor speaks nor stirs;
Ah! what a stricken look was hers!
Deep from within she seems half-way
To lift some weight with sick assay,
And eyes the maid and seeks delay;
Then suddenly, as one defied,
Collects herself in scorn and pride,
And lay down by the Maiden's side!—
And in her arms the maid she took,
    Ah wel-a-day!
And with low voice and doleful look
These words did say:
'In the touch of this bosom there worketh a spell,
Which is lord of thy utterance, Christabel!
Thou knowest to-night, and wilt know to-morrow,
This mark of my shame, this seal of my sorrow;
    But vainly thou warrest,
        For this is alone in
      Thy power to declare,

That in the dim forest
　Thou heard'st a low moaning,
And found'st a bright lady, surpassingly fair;
And didst bring her home with thee in love and in
　charity,
To shield her and shelter her from the damp air.'

The Conclusion to Part I

It was a lovely sight to see
The lady Christabel, when she
Was praying at the old oak tree.
　　Amid the jaggèd shadows
　　Of mossy leafless boughs,
　　Kneeling in the moonlight,
　　To make her gentle vows;
Her slender palms together prest,
Heaving sometimes on her breast;
Her face resigned to bliss or bale—
Her face, oh call it fair not pale,
And both blue eyes more bright than clear,
Each about to have a tear.

With open eyes (ah woe is me!)
Asleep, and dreaming fearfully,
Fearfully dreaming, yet, I wis,
Dreaming that alone, which is—
O sorrow and shame! Can this be she,
The lady, who knelt at the old oak tree?
And lo! the worker of these harms,
That holds the maiden in her arms,
Seems to slumber still and mild,
As a mother with her child.

A star hath set, a star hath risen,
O Geraldine! since arms of thine
Have been the lovely lady's prison.
O Geraldine! one hour was thine—
Thou'st had thy will! By tairn and rill,
The night-birds all that hour were still.
But now they are jubilant anew,
From cliff and tower, tu—whoo! tu—whoo!
Tu—whoo! tu—whoo! from wood and fell!

And see! the lady Christabel
Gathers herself from out her trance;
Her limbs relax, her countenance

Grows sad and soft; the smooth thin lids
Close o'er her eyes; and tears she sheds—
Large tears that leave the lashes bright!
And oft the while she seems to smile
As infants at a sudden light!

Yea, she doth smile, and she doth weep,
Like a youthful hermitess,
Beauteous in a wilderness,
Who, praying always, prays in sleep.
And, if she move unquietly,
Perchance, 'tis but the blood so free
Comes back and tingles in her feet.
No doubt, she hath a vision sweet.
What if her guardian spirit 'twere,
What if she knew her mother near?
But this she knows, in joys and woes,
That saints will aid if men will call:
For the blue sky bends over all!

Part II

Each matin bell, the Baron saith,
Knells us back to a world of death.
These words Sir Leoline first said,
When he rose and found his lady dead:
These words Sir Leoline will say
Many a morn to his dying day!

And hence the custom and law began
That still at dawn the sacristan,
Who duly pulls the heavy bell,
Five and forty beads must tell
Between each stroke—a warning knell,
Which not a soul can choose but hear
From Bratha Head to Wyndermere.

Saith Bracy the bard, So let it knell!
And let the drowsy sacristan
Still count as slowly as he can!
There is no lack of such, I ween,
As well fill up the space between.
In Langdale Pike and Witch's Lair,
And Dungeon-ghyll so foully rent,

With ropes of rock and bells of air
Three sinful sextons' ghosts are pent,
Who all give back, one after t'other,
The death-note to their living brother;
And oft too, by the knell offended,
Just as their one! two! three! is ended,
The devil mocks the doleful tale
With a merry peal from Borodale.

The air is still! through mist and cloud
That merry peal comes ringing loud;
And Geraldine shakes off her dread,
And rises lightly from the bed;
Puts on her silken vestments white,
And tricks her hair in lovely plight,
And nothing doubting of her spell
Awakens the lady Christabel.
'Sleep you, sweet lady Christabel?
I trust that you have rested well.'

And Christabel awoke and spied
The same who lay down by her side—
O rather say, the same whom she
Raised up beneath the old oak tree!

Nay, fairer yet! and yet more fair!
For she belike hath drunken deep
Of all the blessedness of sleep!
And while she spake, her looks, her air
Such gentle thankfulness declare,
That (so it seemed) her girded vests
Grew tight beneath her heaving breasts.
'Sure I have sinn'd!' said Christabel,
'Now heaven be praised if all be well!'

And in low faltering tones, yet sweet,
Did she the lofty lady greet
With such perplexity of mind
As dreams too lively leave behind.

So quickly she rose, and quickly arrayed
Her maiden limbs, and having prayed
That He, who on the cross did groan,
Might wash away her sins unknown,
She forthwith led fair Geraldine
To meet her sire, Sir Leoline.

The lovely maid and the lady tall

Are pacing both into the hall,
And pacing on through page and groom,
Enter the Baron's presence-room.

The Baron rose, and while he prest
His gentle daughter to his breast,
With cheerful wonder in his eyes
The lady Geraldine espies,
And gave such welcome to the same,
As might beseem so bright a dame!

But when he heard the lady's tale,
And when she told her father's name,
Why waxed Sir Leoline so pale,
Murmuring o'er the name again,
Lord Roland de Vaux of Tryermaine?
Alas! they had been friends in youth;
But whispering tongues can poison truth;
And constancy lives in realms above;
And life is thorny; and youth is vain;
And to be wroth with one we love
Doth work like madness in the brain.
And thus it chanced, as I divine,

With Roland and Sir Leoline.
Each spake words of high disdain
And insult to his heart's best brother:
They parted—ne'er to meet again!
But never either found another
To free the hollow heart from paining—
They stood aloof, the scars remaining,
Like cliffs which had been rent asunder;
A dreary sea now flows between;—
But neither heat, nor frost, nor thunder,
Shall wholly do away, I ween,
The marks of that which once hath been.

Sir Leoline, a moment's space,
Stood gazing on the damsel's face:
And the youthful Lord of Tryermaine
Came back upon his heart again.

O then the Baron forgot his age,
His noble heart swelled high with rage;
He swore by the wounds in Jesu's side
He would proclaim it far and wide,
With trump and solemn heraldry,
That they, who thus had wronged the dame,

Were base as spotted infamy!
'And if they dare deny the same,
My herald shall appoint a week,
And let the recreant traitors seek
My tourney court—that there and then
I may dislodge their reptile souls
From the bodies and forms of men!'
He spake: his eye in lightning rolls!
For the lady was ruthlessly seized; and he kenned
In the beautiful lady the child of his friend!

And now the tears were on his face,
And fondly in his arms he took
Fair Geraldine, who met the embrace,
Prolonging it with joyous look.
Which when she viewed, a vision fell
Upon the soul of Christabel,
The vision of fear, the touch and pain!
She shrunk and shuddered, and saw again—
(Ah, woe is me! Was it for thee,
Thou gentle maid! such sights to see?)

Again she saw that bosom old,
Again she felt that bosom cold,

And drew in her breath with a hissing sound:
Whereat the Knight turned wildly round,
And nothing saw, but his own sweet maid
With eyes upraised, as one that prayed.

The touch, the sight, had passed away,
And in its stead that vision blest,
Which comforted her after-rest
While in the lady's arms she lay,
Had put a rapture in her breast,
And on her lips and o'er her eyes
Spread smiles like light!
        With new surprise,
'What ails then my belovèd child?
The Baron said—His daughter mild
Made answer, 'All will yet be well!'
I ween, she had no power to tell
Aught else: so mighty was the spell.

Yet he, who saw this Geraldine,
Had deemed her sure a thing divine:
Such sorrow with such grace she blended,
As if she feared she had offended
Sweet Christabel, that gentle maid!

And with such lowly tones she prayed
She might be sent without delay
Home to her father's mansion.
       'Nay!
Nay, by my soul!' said Leoline.
'Ho! Bracy the bard, the charge be thine!
Go thou, with sweet music and loud,
And take two steeds with trappings proud,
And take the youth whom thou lov'st best
To bear thy harp, and learn thy song,
And clothe you both in solemn vest,
And over the mountains haste along,
Lest wandering folk, that are abroad,
Detain you on the valley road.

'And when he has crossed the Irthing flood,
My merry bard! he hastes, he hastes
Up Knorren Moor, through Halegarth Wood,
And reaches soon that castle good
Which stands and threatens Scotland's wastes.

'Bard Bracy! bard Bracy! your horses are fleet,
Ye must ride up the hall, your music so sweet,
More loud than your horses' echoing feet!

And loud and loud to Lord Roland call,
Thy daughter is safe in Langdale hall!
Thy beautiful daughter is safe and free—
Sir Leoline greets thee thus through me!
He bids thee come without delay
With all thy numerous array
And take thy lovely daughter home:
And he will meet thee on the way
With all his numerous array
White with their panting palfreys' foam:
And, by mine honour! I will say,
That I repent me of the day
When I spake words of fierce disdain
To Roland de Vaux of Tryermaine!—
—For since that evil hour hath flown,
Many a summer's sun hath shone;
Yet ne'er found I a friend again
Like Roland de Vaux of Tryermaine.

The lady fell, and clasped his knees,
Her face upraised, her eyes o'erflowing;
And Bracy replied, with faltering voice,
His gracious Hail on all bestowing!—
'Thy words, thou sire of Christabel,

Are sweeter than my harp can tell;
Yet might I gain a boon of thee,
This day my journey should not be,
So strange a dream hath come to me,
That I had vowed with music loud
To clear yon wood from thing unblest.
Warned by a vision in my rest!
For in my sleep I saw that dove,
That gentle bird, whom thou dost love,
And call'st by thy own daughter's name—
Sir Leoline! I saw the same
Fluttering, and uttering fearful moan,
Among the green herbs in the forest alone.
Which when I saw and when I heard,
I wonder'd what might ail the bird;
For nothing near it could I see
Save the grass and green herbs underneath the old
    tree.

'And in my dream methought I went
To search out what might there be found;
And what the sweet bird's trouble meant,
That thus lay fluttering on the ground.
I went and peered, and could descry

No cause for her distressful cry;
But yet for her dear lady's sake
I stooped, methought, the dove to take,
When lo! I saw a bright green snake
Coiled around its wings and neck.
Green as the herbs on which it couched,
Close by the dove's its head it crouched;
And with the dove it heaves and stirs,
Swelling its neck as she swelled hers!
I woke; it was the midnight hour,
The clock was echoing in the tower;
But though my slumber was gone by,
This dream it would not pass away—
It seems to live upon my eye!

And thence I vowed this self-same day
With music strong and saintly song
To wander through the forest bare,
Lest aught unholy loiter there.'

Thus Bracy said: the Baron, the while,
Half-listening heard him with a smile;
Then turned to Lady Geraldine,
His eyes made up of wonder and love;

And said in courtly accents fine,
'Sweet maid, Lord Roland's beauteous dove,
With arms more strong than harp or song,
Thy sire and I will crush the snake!'
He kissed her forehead as he spake,
And Geraldine in maiden wise
Casting down her large bright eyes,
With blushing cheek and courtesy fine
She turned her from Sir Leoline;
Softly gathering up her train,
That o'er her right arm fell again;
And folded her arms across her chest,
And couched her head upon her breast,
And looked askance at Christabel
Jesu, Maria, shield her well!

A snake's small eye blinks dull and shy;
And the lady's eyes they shrunk in her head,
Each shrunk up to a serpent's eye
And with somewhat of malice, and more of dread,
At Christabel she looked askance!—
One moment—and the sight was fled!
But Christabel in dizzy trance
Stumbling on the unsteady ground

Shuddered aloud, with a hissing sound;
And Geraldine again turned round,
And like a thing, that sought relief,
Full of wonder and full of grief,
She rolled her large bright eyes divine
Wildly on Sir Leoline.

The maid, alas! her thoughts are gone,
She nothing sees—no sight but one!
The maid, devoid of guile and sin,
I know not how, in fearful wise,
So deeply she had drunken in
That look, those shrunken serpent eyes,
That all her features were resigned
To this sole image in her mind:
And passively did imitate
That look of dull and treacherous hate!
And thus she stood, in dizzy trance;
Still picturing that look askance
With forced unconscious sympathy
Full before her father's view—
As far as such a look could be
In eyes so innocent and blue!

And when the trance was o'er, the maid
Paused awhile, and inly prayed:
Then falling at the Baron's feet,
'By my mother's soul do I entreat
That thou this woman send away!'
She said: and more she could not say:
For what she knew she could not tell,
O'er-mastered by the mighty spell.

Why is thy cheek so wan and wild,
Sir Leoline? Thy only child
Lies at thy feet, thy joy, thy pride,
So fair, so innocent, so mild;
The same, for whom thy lady died!
O by the pangs of her dear mother
Think thou no evil of thy child!
For her, and thee, and for no other,
She prayed the moment ere she died:
Prayed that the babe for whom she died,
Might prove her dear lord's joy and pride!
    That prayer her deadly pangs beguiled,
        Sir Leoline!
    And wouldst thou wrong thy only child,
        Her child and thine?

Within the Baron's heart and brain
If thoughts, like these, had any share,
They only swelled his rage and pain,
And did but work confusion there.
His heart was cleft with pain and rage,
His cheeks they quivered, his eyes were wild,
Dishonoured thus in his old age;
Dishonoured by his only child,
And all his hospitality
To the wronged daughter of his friend
By more than woman's jealousy
Brought thus to a disgraceful end—
He rolled his eye with stern regard
Upon the gentle minstrel bard,
And said in tones abrupt, austere—
'Why, Bracy! dost thou loiter here?
I bade thee hence!' The bard obeyed;
And turning from his own sweet maid,
The agèd knight, Sir Leoline,
Led forth the lady Geraldine!

The Conclusion to Part II

A little child, a limber elf,
Singing, dancing to itself,
A fairy thing with red round cheeks,
That always finds, and never seeks,
Makes such a vision to the sight
As fills a father's eyes with light;
And pleasures flow in so thick and fast
Upon his heart, that he at last
Must needs express his love's excess
With words of unmeant bitterness.
Perhaps 'tis pretty to force together
Thoughts so all unlike each other;
To mutter and mock a broken charm,
To dally with wrong that does no harm.
Perhaps 'tis tender too and pretty
At each wild word to feel within
A sweet recoil of love and pity.
And what, if in a world of sin
(O sorrow and shame should this be true!)
Such giddiness of heart and brain
Comes seldom save from rage and pain,
So talks as it 's most used to do.

Lord Byron
(1788–1824)

And Thou art Dead, as Young and Fair

And thou art dead, as young and fair
As aught of mortal birth;
And form so soft, and charms so rare,
Too soon return'd to Earth!
Though Earth receiv'd them in her bed,
And o'er the spot the crowd may tread
In carelessness or mirth,
There is an eye which could not brook
A moment on that grave to look.

I will not ask where thou liest low,
Nor gaze upon the spot;
There flowers or weeds at will may grow,
So I behold them not:
It is enough for me to prove
That what I lov'd, and long must love,

Like common earth can rot;
To me there needs no stone to tell,
'T is Nothing that I lov'd so well.

Yet did I love thee to the last
As fervently as thou,
Who didst not change through all the past,
And canst not alter now.
The love where Death has set his seal,
Nor age can chill, nor rival steal,
Nor falsehood disavow:
And, what were worse, thou canst not see
Or wrong, or change, or fault in me.

The better days of life were ours;
The worst can be but mine:
The sun that cheers, the storm that lowers,
Shall never more be thine.
The silence of that dreamless sleep
I envy now too much to weep;
Nor need I to repine
That all those charms have pass'd away,
I might have watch'd through long decay.

The flower in ripen'd bloom unmatch'd
Must fall the earliest prey;
Though by no hand untimely snatch'd,
The leaves must drop away:
And yet it were a greater grief
To watch it withering, leaf by leaf,
Than see it pluck'd to-day;
Since earthly eye but ill can bear
To trace the change to foul from fair.

I know not if I could have borne
To see thy beauties fade;
The night that follow'd such a morn
Had worn a deeper shade:
Thy day without a cloud hath pass'd,
And thou wert lovely to the last,
Extinguish'd, not decay'd;
As stars that shoot along the sky
Shine brightest as they fall from high.

As once I wept, if I could weep,
My tears might well be shed,
To think I was not near to keep
One vigil o'er thy bed;

To gaze, how fondly! on thy face,
To fold thee in a faint embrace,
Uphold thy drooping head;
And show that love, however vain,
Nor thou nor I can feel again.

Yet how much less it were to gain,
Though thou hast left me free,
The loveliest things that still remain,
Than thus remember thee!
The all of thine that cannot die
Through dark and dread Eternity
Returns again to me,
And more thy buried love endears
Than aught except its living years.

When We Two Parted

When we two parted
    In silence and tears,
Half broken-hearted
    To sever for years,
Pale grew thy cheek and cold,
    Colder thy kiss;
Truly that hour foretold
    Sorrow to this.

The dew of the morning
    Sunk chill on my brow—
It felt like the warning
    Of what I feel now.
Thy vows are all broken,
    And light is thy fame;
I hear thy name spoken,
    And share in its shame.

They name thee before me,
    A knell to mine ear;
A shudder comes o'er me—
    Why wert thou so dear?

They know not I knew thee,
    Who knew thee too well—
Long, long shall I rue thee,
    Too deeply to tell.

In secret we met—
    In silence I grieve,
That thy heart could forget,
    Thy spirit deceive.
If I should meet thee
    After long years,
How should I greet thee?—
    With silence and tears.

Percy Bysshe Shelley
(1792–1822)

The Cold Earth Slept Below

The cold earth slept below;
    Above the cold sky shone;
      And all around,
      With a chilling sound,
From caves of ice and fields of snow
The breath of night like death did flow
      Beneath the sinking moon.

The wintry hedge was black;
    The green grass was not seen;
      The birds did rest
      On the bare thorn's breast,
Whose roots, beside the pathway track,
Had bound their folds o'er many a crack
      Which the frost had made between.

Thine eyes glow'd in the glare
    Of the moon's dying light;
        As a fen-fire's beam
        On a sluggish stream
Gleams dimly—so the moon shone there,
And it yellow'd the strings of thy tangled hair,
        That shook in the wind of night.

The moon made thy lips pale, beloved;
    The wind made thy bosom chill;
        The night did shed
        On thy dear head
Its frozen dew, and thou didst lie
Where the bitter breath of the naked sky
        Might visit thee at will.

John Clare
(1793–1864)

An Invite, to Eternity

Wilt thou go with me, sweet maid,
Say, maiden, wilt thou go with me
Through the valley-depths of shade,
Of night and dark obscurity;
Where the path has lost its way,
Where the sun forgets the day,
Where there's nor life nor light to see,
Sweet maiden, wilt thou go with me!

Where stones will turn to flooding streams,
Where plains will rise like ocean waves,
Where life will fade like visioned dreams
And mountains darken into caves,
Say, maiden, wilt thou go with me
Through this sad non-identity,

Where parents live and are forgot,
And sisters live and know us not!

Say, maiden; wilt thou go with me
In this strange death of life to be,
To live in death and be the same,
Without this life or home or name,
At once to be and not to be -
That was and is not -yet to see
Things pass like shadows, and the sky
Above, below, around us lie?

The land of shadows wilt thou trace
And look nor know each other's face.
The present mixed with reasons gone,
And past and present all as one.
Say maiden, can thy life be led
To join the living to the dead?
Then trace thy footsteps on with me,
We're wed to one eternity.

John Keats
(1795–1821)

La Belle Dame sans Merci

O what can ail thee, knight-at-arms,
   Alone and palely loitering?
The sedge has withered from the lake,
   And no birds sing!

O what can ail thee, knight-at-arms,
   So haggard and so woe-begone?
The squirrel's granary is full,
   And the harvest's done.

I see a lily on thy brow,
   With anguish moist and fever-dew,
And on thy cheeks a fading rose
   Fast withereth too.

I met a lady in the meads,
    Full beautiful, a fairy's child;
Her hair was long, her foot was light,
    And her eyes were wild.

I made a garland for her head,
    And bracelets too, and fragrant zone;
She looked at me as she did love,
    And made sweet moan.

I set her on my pacing steed,
    And nothing else saw all day long,
For sidelong would she bend, and sing
    A faery's song.

She found me roots of relish sweet,
    And honey wild, and manna-dew,
And sure in language strange she said—
    'I love thee true'.

She took me to her Elfin grot,
    And there she wept and sighed full sore,
And there I shut her wild, wild eyes
    With kisses four.

And there she lullèd me asleep,
  And there I dreamed—Ah! woe betide!—
The latest dream I ever dreamt
  On the cold hill side.

I saw pale kings and princes too,
  Pale warriors, death-pale were they all;
They cried—'La Belle Dame sans Merci
  Hath thee in thrall!'

I saw their starved lips in the gloam,
  With horrid warning gapèd wide,
And I awoke and found me here,
  On the cold hill's side.

And this is why I sojourn here,
  Alone and palely loitering,
Though the sedge is withered from the lake,
  And no birds sing.

Bright Star, Would I
Were Stedfast as Thou Art

Bright star, would I were stedfast as thou art—
    Not in lone splendour hung aloft the night
And watching, with eternal lids apart,
    Like nature's patient, sleepless Eremite,
The moving waters at their priestlike task
    Of pure ablution round earth's human shores,
Or gazing on the new soft-fallen mask
    Of snow upon the mountains and the moors—
No—yet still stedfast, still unchangeable,
    Pillow'd upon my fair love's ripening breast,
To feel for ever its soft fall and swell,
    Awake for ever in a sweet unrest,
Still, still to hear her tender-taken breath,
And so live ever—or else swoon to death.

Elizabeth Barrett Browning
(1806–1861)

Sonnet 28

My letters! all dead paper, . . . mute and white!—
And yet they seem alive and quivering
Against my tremulous hands which loose the string
And let them drop down on my knee to-night.
This said, . . . he wished to have me in his sight
Once, as a friend: this fixed a day in spring
To come and touch my hand . . . a simple thing,
Yet I wept for it! — this, . . . the paper's light . . .
Said, *Dear, I love thee*; and I sank and quailed
As if God's future thundered on my past.
This said, *I am thine*—and so its ink has paled
With lying at my heart that beat too fast.
And this . . . O Love, thy words have ill availed,
If, what this said, I dared repeat at last!

Sonnet 43

How do I love thee? Let me count the ways.
I love thee to the depth and breadth and height
My soul can reach, when feeling out of sight
For the ends of being and ideal grace.
I love thee to the level of every day's
Most quiet need, by sun and candle-light.
I love thee freely, as men strive for right.
I love thee purely, as they turn from praise.
I love thee with the passion put to use
In my old griefs, and with my childhood's faith.
I love thee with a love I seemed to lose
With my lost saints. I love thee with the breath,
Smiles, tears, of all my life; and, if God choose,
I shall but love thee better after death.

Edgar Allan Poe
(1809–1849)

Lenore

Ah, broken is the golden bowl! the spirit flown forever!
Let the bell toll!—a saintly soul floats on the Stygian river.
And, Guy de Vere, hast *thou* no tear?—weep now or never more!
See! on yon drear and rigid bier low lies thy love, Lenore!
Come! let the burial rite be read—the funeral song be sung!—
An anthem for the queenliest dead that ever died so young—
A dirge for her, the doubly dead in that she died so young.

"Wretches! ye loved her for her wealth and hated her for her pride,
And when she fell in feeble health, ye blessed her—that she died!
How *shall* the ritual, then, be read?—the requiem how be sung
By you—by yours, the evil eye,—by yours, the slanderous tongue
That did to death the innocence that died, and died so young?"

Peccavimus; but rave not thus! and let a Sabbath song
Go up to God so solemnly the dead may feel no wrong!
The sweet Lenore hath "gone before," with Hope, that flew beside,
Leaving thee wild for the dear child that should have been thy bride—
For her, the fair and *débonnaire*, that now so lowly lies,
The life upon her yellow hair but not within her eyes—
The life still there, upon her hair—the death upon her eyes.

"Avaunt! to-night my heart is light. No dirge will I upraise,
But waft the angel on her flight with a pæan of old days!
Let *no* bell toll!—lest her sweet soul, amid its hallowed mirth,
Should catch the note, as it doth float up from the damned Earth.
To friends above, from fiends below, the indignant ghost is riven—
From Hell unto a high estate far up within the Heaven—
From grief and groan to a golden throne beside the King of Heaven."

The Haunted Palace

In the greenest of our valleys
By good angels tenanted,
Once a fair and stately palace—
Radiant palace—reared its head.
In the monarch Thought's dominion,
It stood there!
Never seraph spread a pinion
Over fabric half so fair!

Banners yellow, glorious, golden,
On its roof did float and flow
(This—all this—was in the olden
Time long ago)
And every gentle air that dallied,
In that sweet day,
Along the ramparts plumed and pallid,
A wingèd odor went away.

Wanderers in that happy valley,
Through two luminous windows, saw
Spirits moving musically
To a lute's well-tunèd law,

Round about a throne where, sitting,
Porphyrogene!
In state his glory well befitting,
The ruler of the realm was seen.

And all with pearl and ruby glowing
Was the fair palace door,
Through which came flowing, flowing, flowing
And sparkling evermore,
A troop of Echoes, whose sweet duty
Was but to sing,
In voices of surpassing beauty,
The wit and wisdom of their king.

But evil things, in robes of sorrow,
Assailed the monarch's high estate;
(Ah, let us mourn!—for never morrow
Shall dawn upon him, desolate!)
And round about his home the glory
That blushed and bloomed
Is but a dim-remembered story
Of the old time entombed.

And travellers, now, within that valley,
Through the red-litten windows see
Vast forms that move fantastically
To a discordant melody;
While, like a ghastly rapid river,
Through the pale door
A hideous throng rush out forever,
And laugh—but smile no more.

The Raven

Once upon a midnight dreary, while I pondered, weak and weary,
Over many a quaint and curious volume of forgotten lore—
    While I nodded, nearly napping, suddenly there came a tapping,
As of some one gently rapping, rapping at my chamber door.
"'Tis some visitor," I muttered, "tapping at my chamber door—
      Only this and nothing more."

    Ah, distinctly I remember it was in the bleak December;
And each separate dying ember wrought its ghost upon the floor.
    Eagerly I wished the morrow;—vainly I had sought to borrow
    From my books surcease of sorrow—sorrow for the lost Lenore—
For the rare and radiant maiden whom the angels name Lenore—
      Nameless *here* for evermore.

    And the silken, sad, uncertain rustling of each purple curtain
Thrilled me—filled me with fantastic terrors never felt before;
    So that now, to still the beating of my heart, I stood repeating
    "'Tis some visitor entreating entrance at my chamber door—
Some late visitor entreating entrance at my chamber door;—
      This it is and nothing more."

Presently my soul grew stronger; hesitating then no longer,
"Sir," said I, "or Madam, truly your forgiveness I implore;
    But the fact is I was napping, and so gently you came rapping,
    And so faintly you came tapping, tapping at my chamber door,
That I scarce was sure I heard you"—here I opened wide the door;—
        Darkness there and nothing more.

Deep into that darkness peering, long I stood there wondering,
        fearing,
Doubting, dreaming dreams no mortal ever dared to dream before;
    But the silence was unbroken, and the stillness gave no token,
    And the only word there spoken was the whispered word,
        "Lenore?"
This I whispered, and an echo murmured back the word, "Lenore!"—
        Merely this and nothing more.

Back into the chamber turning, all my soul within me burning,
Soon again I heard a tapping somewhat louder than before.
    "Surely," said I, "surely that is something at my window lattice;
    Let me see, then, what thereat is, and this mystery explore—
Let my heart be still a moment and this mystery explore;—
        'Tis the wind and nothing more!"

Open here I flung the shutter, when, with many a flirt and flutter,
In there stepped a stately Raven of the saintly days of yore;
 Not the least obeisance made he; not a minute stopped or
  stayed he;
 But, with mien of lord or lady, perched above my chamber door—
Perched upon a bust of Pallas just above my chamber door—
  Perched, and sat, and nothing more.

Then this ebony bird beguiling my sad fancy into smiling,
By the grave and stern decorum of the countenance it wore,
"Though thy crest be shorn and shaven, thou," I said, "art sure no
 craven,
Ghastly grim and ancient Raven wandering from the Nightly
 shore—
Tell me what thy lordly name is on the Night's Plutonian shore!"
  Quoth the Raven "Nevermore."

Much I marvelled this ungainly fowl to hear discourse so plainly,
Though its answer little meaning—little relevancy bore;
 For we cannot help agreeing that no living human being
  Ever yet was blessed with seeing bird above his chamber door—
Bird or beast upon the sculptured bust above his chamber door,
  With such name as "Nevermore."

But the Raven, sitting lonely on the placid bust, spoke only

That one word, as if his soul in that one word he did outpour.

    Nothing farther then he uttered—not a feather then he fluttered—

    Till I scarcely more than muttered "Other friends have flown

        before—

On the morrow *he* will leave me, as my Hopes have flown before."

        Then the bird said "Nevermore."

    Startled at the stillness broken by reply so aptly spoken,

"Doubtless," said I, "what it utters is its only stock and store

    Caught from some unhappy master whom unmerciful Disaster

    Followed fast and followed faster till his songs one burden bore—

Till the dirges of his Hope that melancholy burden bore

        Of 'Never—nevermore'."

    But the Raven still beguiling all my fancy into smiling,

Straight I wheeled a cushioned seat in front of bird, and bust

    and door;

    Then, upon the velvet sinking, I betook myself to linking

    Fancy unto fancy, thinking what this ominous bird of yore—

What this grim, ungainly, ghastly, gaunt, and ominous bird of yore

        Meant in croaking "Nevermore."

This I sat engaged in guessing, but no syllable expressing
To the fowl whose fiery eyes now burned into my bosom's core;
This and more I sat divining, with my head at ease reclining
On the cushion's velvet lining that the lamp-light gloated o'er,
But whose velvet-violet lining with the lamp-light gloating o'er,
    She shall press, ah, nevermore!

Then, methought, the air grew denser, perfumed from an unseen
  censer
Swung by Seraphim whose foot-falls tinkled on the tufted floor.
"Wretch," I cried, "thy God hath lent thee—by these angels he
  hath sent thee
Respite—respite and nepenthe from thy memories of Lenore;
Quaff, oh quaff this kind nepenthe and forget this lost Lenore!"
    Quoth the Raven "Nevermore."

"Prophet!" said I, "thing of evil!—prophet still, if bird or devil!—
Whether Tempter sent, or whether tempest tossed thee here ashore,
Desolate yet all undaunted, on this desert land enchanted—
On this home by Horror haunted—tell me truly, I implore—
Is there—*is* there balm in Gilead?—tell me—tell me, I implore!"
    Quoth the Raven "Nevermore."

"Prophet!" said I, "thing of evil!—prophet still, if bird or devil!
By that Heaven that bends above us—by that God we both adore—
   Tell this soul with sorrow laden if, within the distant Aidenn,
   It shall clasp a sainted maiden whom the angels name Lenore—
Clasp a rare and radiant maiden whom the angels name Lenore."
       Quoth the Raven "Nevermore."

"Be that word our sign of parting, bird or fiend!" I shrieked,
    upstarting—
"Get thee back into the tempest and the Night's Plutonian shore!
   Leave no black plume as a token of that lie thy soul hath spoken!
   Leave my loneliness unbroken!—quit the bust above my door!
Take thy beak from out my heart, and take thy form from off my
   door!"
       Quoth the Raven "Nevermore."

And the Raven, never flitting, still is sitting, *still* is sitting
On the pallid bust of Pallas just above my chamber door;
   And his eyes have all the seeming of a demon's that is dreaming,
   And the lamp-light o'er him streaming throws his shadow on
    the floor;
And my soul from out that shadow that lies floating on the floor
    Shall be lifted—nevermore!

A Dream Within a Dream

Take this kiss upon the brow!
And, in parting from you now,
Thus much let me avow —
You are not wrong, who deem
That my days have been a dream;
Yet if hope has flown away
In a night, or in a day,
In a vision, or in none,
Is it therefore the less *gone*?
All that we see or seem
Is but a dream within a dream.

I stand amid the roar
Of a surf-tormented shore,
And I hold within my hand
Grains of the golden sand —
How few! yet how they creep
Through my fingers to the deep,
While I weep — while I weep!
O God! Can I not grasp

Them with a tighter clasp?
O God! can I not save
One from the pitiless wave?
Is *all* that we see or seem
But a dream within a dream?

Annabel Lee

It was many and many a year ago,
    In a kingdom by the sea
That a maiden there lived whom you may know
    By the name of ANNABEL LEE;
And this maiden she lived with no other thought
    Than to love and be loved by me.

I was a child and *she* was a child,
    In this kingdom by the sea.
But we loved with a love that was more than love—
    I and my ANNABEL LEE—
With a love that the wingëd seraphs of heaven
    Coveted her and me.

And this was the reason that, long ago,
    In this kingdom by the sea,
A wind blew out of a cloud, chilling
    My beautiful ANNABEL LEE;
So that her highborn kinsmen came
    And bore her away from me,
To shut her up in a sepulchre
    In this kingdom by the sea.

The angels, not half so happy in heaven,
    Went envying her and me—
Yes!—that was the reason (as all men know,
    In this kingdom by the sea)
That the wind came out of the cloud by night,
    Chilling and killing my ANNABEL LEE.

But our love it was stronger by far than the love
    Of those who were older than we—
    Of many far wiser than we—
And neither the angels in heaven above,
    Nor the demons down under the sea,
Can ever dissever my soul from the soul
    Of the beautiful ANNABEL LEE:

For the moon never beams, without bringing me dreams
    Of the beautiful ANNABEL LEE;
And the stars never rise but I feel the bright eyes
    Of the beautiful ANNABEL LEE,
And so, all the night-tide, I lie down by the side
Of my darling—my darling—my life and my bride,
    In her sepulchre there by the sea—
    In her tomb by the sounding sea.

Alfred Tennyson
(1809–1892)

The Lady of Shalott

Part the First

On either side the river lie
Long fields of barley and of rye,
That clothe the wold, and meet the sky.
And thro' the field the road runs by
    To manytowered Camelot.
The yellowleavèd waterlily,
The green-sheathèd daffodilly,
Tremble in the water chilly,
    Round about Shalott.

Willows whiten, aspens shiver,
The sunbeam-showers break and quiver
In the stream that runneth ever
By the island in the river,
    Flowing down to Camelot.
Four gray walls, and four gray towers
Overlook a space of flowers,
And the silent isle imbowers
    The Lady of Shalott.

Underneath the bearded barley,
The reaper, reaping late and early,
Hears her ever chanting cheerly,
Like an angel, singing clearly,
    O'er the stream of Camelot.
Piling the sheaves in furrows airy,
Beneath the moon, the reaper weary
Listening whispers, "'tis the fairy
    Lady of Shalott."

The little isle is all inrailed
With a rose-fence, and overtrailed
With roses: by the marge unhailed
The shallop flitteth silkensailed,
    Skimming down to Camelot.
A pearlgarland winds her head:
She leaneth on a velvet bed,
Full royally apparellèd,
    The Lady of Shalott.

Part the Second

No time hath she to sport and play:
A charmèd web she weaves alway.
A curse is on her, if she stay
Her weaving, either night or day,
    To look down to Camelot.

She knows not what the curse may be;
Therefore she weaveth steadily,
Therefore no other care hath she,
    The Lady of Shalott.

She lives with little joy or fear.
Over the water, running near,
The sheepbell tinkles in her ear.
Before her hangs a mirror clear,
    Reflecting tower'd Camelot.
And as the mazy web she whirls,
She sees the surly village churls,
And the red cloaks of market-girls,
    Pass onward from Shalott.

Sometimes a troop of damsels glad,
An abbot on an ambling pad,
Sometimes a curly shepherd lad,
Or longhair'd page in crimson clad,
    Goes by to towered Camelot.

And sometimes thro' the mirror blue,
The knights come riding, two and two.
She hath no loyal knight and true,
    The Lady of Shalott.

But in her web she still delights
To weave the mirror's magic sights:
For often thro' the silent nights
A funeral, with plumes and lights
    And music, came from Camelot.
Or, when the moon was overhead,
Came two young lovers, lately wed:
"I am half-sick of shadows," said
    The Lady of Shalott.

Part the Third

A bowshot from her bower-eaves.
He rode between the barley-sheaves:
The sun came dazzling thro' the leaves,
And flamed upon the brazen greaves
    Of bold Sir Lancelot.
A redcross knight for ever kneeled
To a lady in his shield,
That sparkled on the yellow field,
    Beside remote Shalott.

The gemmy bridle glittered free,
Like to some branch of stars we see
Hung in the golden Galaxy.
The bridle-bells rang merrily,
    As he rode down from Camelot.

And from his blazon'd baldric slung,
A mighty silver bugle hung,
And, as he rode, his armour rung,
    Beside remote Shalott.

All in the blue unclouded weather,
Thickjewelled shone the saddle-leather.
The helmet, and the helmet-feather
Burned like one burning flame together,
    As he rode down from Camelot.
As often thro' the purple night,
Below the starry clusters bright,
Some bearded meteor, trailing light,
    Moves over green Shalott.

His broad clear brow in sunlight glowed.
On burnished hooves his war-horse trode.
From underneath his helmet flowed
His coalblack curls, as on he rode,
 As he rode down from Camelot.
From the bank, and from the river,
He flashed into the crystal mirror,
"Tirra lirra, tirra lirra,"
 Sang Sir Lancelot.

She left the web: she left the loom:
She made three paces thro' the room:
She saw the waterflower bloom:
She saw the helmet and the plume:
 She looked down to Camelot.
Out flew the web, and floated wide,
The mirror cracked from side to side,
"The curse is come upon me," cried
 The Lady of Shalott.

Part the Fourth

In the stormy eastwind straining
The pale-yellow woods were waning,
The broad stream in his banks complaining,
Heavily the low sky raining
    Over towered Camelot:
Outside the isle a shallow boat
Beneath a willow lay afloat,
Below the carven stern she wrote,
    THE LADY OF SHALOTT.

A cloudwhite crown of pearl she dight.
All raimented in snowy white
That loosely flew, (her zone in sight,
Clasped with one blinding diamond bright,)
    Her wide eyes fixed on Camelot,
Though the squally eastwind keenly
Blew, with folded arms serenely
By the water stood the queenly
    Lady of Shalott.

With a steady, stony glance—
Like some bold seer in a trance,
Beholding all his own mischance,
Mute, with a glassy countenance—
    She looked down to Camelot.
It was the closing of the day,
She loosed the chain, and down she lay,
The broad stream bore her far away,
    The Lady of Shalott.

As when to sailors while they roam,
By creeks and outfalls far from home,
Rising and dropping with the foam,
From dying swans wild warblings come,
    Blown shoreward; so to Camelot

Still as the boathead wound along
The willowy hills and fields among,
They heard her chanting her deathsong,
    The Lady of Shalott.

A longdrawn carol, mournful, holy,
She chanted loudly, chanted lowly,
Till her eyes were darkened wholly,
And her smooth face sharpened slowly
    Turned to towered Camelot:
For ere she reach'd upon the tide
The first house by the waterside,
Singing in her song she died,
    The Lady of Shalott.

Under tower and balcony,
By gardenwall and gallery,
A pale, pale corpse she floated by,
Deadcold, between the houses high,
    Dead into towered Camelot.

Knight and burgher, lord and dame,
To the plankèd wharfage came:
Below the stern they read her name,
    "The Lady of Shalott."

They cross'd themselves, their stars they blest,
Knight, minstrel, abbot, squire and guest.
There lay a parchment on her breast,
That puzzled more than all the rest,
    The wellfed wits at Camelot.
"*The web was woven curiously*
The charm is broken utterly,
Draw near and fear not,—this is I,
    The Lady of Shalott."

Emily Brontë
(1818–1848)

Spellbound

The night is darkening round me,
The wild winds coldly blow;
But a tyrant spell has bound me
And I cannot, cannot go.

The giant trees are bending
Their bare boughs weighed with snow.
And the storm is fast descending,
And yet I cannot go.

Clouds beyond clouds above me,
Wastes beyond wastes below;
But nothing drear can move me;
I will not, cannot go.

Remembrance

Cold in the earth—and the deep snow piled above thee,
Far, far removed, cold in the dreary grave!
Have I forgot, my only Love, to love thee,
Severed at last by Time's all-severing wave?

Now, when alone, do my thoughts no longer hover
Over the mountains, on that northern shore,
Resting their wings where heath and fern-leaves cover
Thy noble heart forever, ever more?

Cold in the earth—and fifteen wild Decembers,
From those brown hills, have melted into spring:
Faithful, indeed, is the spirit that remembers
After such years of change and suffering!

Sweet Love of youth, forgive, if I forget thee,
While the world's tide is bearing me along;
Other desires and other hopes beset me,
Hopes which obscure, but cannot do thee wrong!

No later light has lightened up my heaven,
No second morn has ever shone for me;
All my life's bliss from thy dear life was given,
All my life's bliss is in the grave with thee.

But, when the days of golden dreams had perished,
And even Despair was powerless to destroy,
Then did I learn how existence could be cherished,
Strengthened, and fed without the aid of joy.

Then did I check the tears of useless passion—
Weaned my young soul from yearning after thine;
Sternly denied its burning wish to hasten
Down to that tomb already more than mine.

And, even yet, I dare not let it languish,
Dare not indulge in memory's rapturous pain;
Once drinking deep of that divinest anguish,
How could I seek the empty world again?

Charles Baudelaire
(1821–1867)

A Carcass

Recall to mind the sight we saw, my soul,
    That soft, sweet summer day:
Upon a bed of flints a carrion foul,
    Just as we turn'd the way,

Its legs erected, wanton-like, in air.
    Burning and sweating pest.
In unconcern'd and cynic sort laid bare
    To view its noisome breast.

The sun lit up the rottenness with gold,
    To bake it well inclined,
And give great Nature back a hundredfold
    All she together join'd.

The sky regarded as the carcass proud
   Oped flower-like to the day;
So strong the odour, on the grass you vow'd
   You thought to faint away.

The flies the putrid belly buzz'd about,
   Whence black battalions throng
Of maggots, like thick liquid flowing out
   The living rags along.

And as a wave they mounted and went down.
   Or darted sparkling wide;
As if the body, by a wild breath blown,
   Lived as it multiplied.

From all this life a music strange there ran.
   Like wind and running burns;
Or like the wheat a winnower in his fan
   With rhythmic movement turns.

The forms wore off, and as a dream grew faint,
   An outline dimly shown.
And which the artist finishes to paint
   From memory alone.

Behind the rocks watch'd us with angry eye
    A bitch disturb'd in theft,
"Waiting to take, till we had pass'd her by,
    The morsel she had left.

Yet you will be like that corruption too,
    Like that infection prove—
Star of my eyes, sun of my nature, you,
    My angel and my love!

Queen of the graces, you will even be so,
    When, the last ritual said,
Beneath the grass and the fat flowers you go,
    To mould among the dead.

Then, O my beauty, tell the insatiate worm,
    Who wastes you with his kiss,
I have kept the godlike essence and the form
    Of perishable bliss!

The Ghost

Softly as brown-eyed Angels rove
I will return to thy alcove,
And glide upon the night to thee,
Treading the shadows silently.

And I will give to thee, my own,
Kisses as icy as the moon,
And the caresses of a snake
Cold gliding in the thorny brake.

And when returns the livid morn
Thou shalt find all my place forlorn
And chilly, till the falling night.

Others would rule by tenderness
Over thy life and youthfulness,
But I would conquer thee by fright!

The Death of Lovers

There shall be couches whence faint odours rise,
Divans like sepulchres, deep and profound;
Strange flowers that bloomed beneath diviner skies
The death-bed of our love shall breathe around.

And guarding their last embers till the end,
Our hearts shall be the torches of the shrine,
And their two leaping flames shall fade and blend
In the twin mirrors of your soul and mine.

And through the eve of rose and mystic blue
A beam of love shall pass from me to you,
Like a long sigh charged with a last farewell;

And later still an angel, flinging wide
The gates, shall bring to life with joyful spell
The tarnished mirrors and the flames that died.

Christina Rossetti
(1830–1894)

After Death

The curtains were half drawn, the floor was swept
And strewn with rushes, rosemary and may
Lay thick upon the bed on which I lay,
Where through the lattice ivy-shadows crept.
He leaned above me, thinking that I slept
And could not hear him; but I heard him say,
'Poor child, poor child': and as he turned away
Came a deep silence, and I knew he wept.
He did not touch the shroud, or raise the fold
That hid my face, or take my hand in his,
Or ruffle the smooth pillows for my head:
He did not love me living; but once dead
He pitied me; and very sweet it is
To know he still is warm though I am cold.

Echo

Come to me in the silence of the night;
  Come in the speaking silence of a dream;
Come with soft rounded cheeks and eyes as bright
    As sunlight on a stream;
      Come back in tears,
O memory, hope, love of finished years.

Oh dream how sweet, too sweet, too bitter sweet,
  Whose wakening should have been in Paradise,
Where souls brimfull of love abide and meet;
    Where thirsting longing eyes
      Watch the slow door
That opening, letting in, lets out no more.

Yet come to me in dreams, that I may live
  My very life again though cold in death:
Come back to me in dreams, that I may give
    Pulse for pulse, breath for breath:
      Speak low, lean low,
As long ago, my love, how long ago!

Song

When I am dead, my dearest,
  Sing no sad songs for me;
Plant thou no roses at my head,
  Nor shady cypress tree:
Be the green grass above me
  With showers and dewdrops wet;
And if thou wilt, remember,
  And if thou wilt, forget.

I shall not see the shadows,
  I shall not feel the rain;
I shall not hear the nightingale
  Sing on, as if in pain:
And dreaming through the twilight
  That doth not rise nor set,
Haply I may remember,
  And haply may forget.

Jessie Cameron

"Jessie, Jessie Cameron,
    Hear me but this once," quoth he.
"Good luck go with you, neighbor's son,
    But I'm no mate for you," quoth she.
Day was verging toward the night
    There beside the moaning sea,
Dimness overtook the light
    There where the breakers be.
"O Jessie, Jessie Cameron,
    I have loved you long and true."—
"Good luck go with you, neighbor's son,
    But I'm no mate for you."

She was a careless, fearless girl,
    And made her answer plain;
Outspoken she to earl or churl,
    Kind-hearted in the main,
But somewhat heedless with her tongue,
    And apt at causing pain;
A mirthful maiden she and young,
    Most fair for bliss or bane.
"O, long ago I told you so,

I tell you so to-day:
Go you your way, and let me go
   Just my own free way."

The sea swept in with moan and foam
   Quickening the stretch of sand;
They stood almost in sight of home;
   He strove to take her hand.
"O, can't you take your answer then,
   And won't you understand?
For me you're not the man of men,
   I've other plans are planned.
You're good for Madge, or good for Cis,
   Or good for Kate, may be:
But what's to me the good of this
   While you're not good for me?"

They stood together on the beach,
   They two alone,
And louder waxed his urgent speech,
   His patience almost gone:
"O, say but one kind word to me,
   Jessie, Jessie Cameron."—
"I'd be too proud to beg," quoth she,

And pride was in her tone.
And pride was in her lifted head,
  And in her angry eye,
And in her foot, which might have fled,
  But would not fly.

Some say that he had gypsy blood,
  That in his heart was guile:
Yet he had gone through fire and flood
  Only to win her smile.
Some say his grandam was a witch,
  A black witch from beyond the Nile,
Who kept an image in a niche
  And talked with it the while.
And by her hut far down the lane
  Some say they would not pass at night,
Lest they should hear an unked strain
  Or see an unked sight.

Alas, for Jessie Cameron!—
  The sea crept moaning, moaning nigher:
She should have hastened to be gone,—
  The sea swept higher, breaking by her:
She should have hastened to her home

While yet the west was flushed with fire,
But now her feet are in the foam,
 The sea-foam, sweeping higher.
O mother, linger at your door,
 And light your lamp to make it plain;
But Jessie she comes home no more,
 No more again.

They stood together on the strand,
 They only, each by each;
Home, her home, was close at hand,
 Utterly out of reach.
Her mother in the chimney nook
 Heard a startled sea-gull screech,
But never turned her head to look
 Towards the darkening beach:
Neighbors here and neighbors there
 Heard one scream, as if a bird
Shrilly screaming cleft the air:—
 That was all they heard.

Jessie she comes home no more,
 Comes home never;
Her lover's step sounds at his door

No more forever.
And boats may search upon the sea
    And search along the river,
But none know where the bodies be:
    Sea-winds that shiver,
Sea-birds that breast the blast,
    Sea-waves swelling,
Keep the secret first and last
    Of their dwelling.

Whether the tide so hemmed them round
    With its pitiless flow,
That when they would have gone they found
    No way to go;
Whether she scorned him to the last
    With words flung to and fro,
Or clung to him when hope was past,
    None will ever know:
Whether he helped or hindered her,
    Threw up his life or lost it well,
The troubled sea, for all its stir,
    Finds no voice to tell.

Only watchers by the dying
   Have thought they heard one pray,
Wordless, urgent; and replying,
   One seem to say him nay:
And watchers by the dead have heard
   A windy swell from miles away,
With sobs and screams, but not a word
   Distinct for them to say:
And watchers out at sea have caught
   Glimpse of a pale gleam here or there,
Come and gone as quick as thought,
   Which might be hand or hair.

Thomas Hardy
(1840–1928)

A Sign-Seeker

I MARK the months in liveries dank and dry,
    The day-tides many-shaped and hued;
    I see the nightfall shades subtrude,
And hear the monotonous hours clang negligently by.

I view the evening bonfires of the sun
    On hills where morning rains have hissed;
    The eyeless countenance of the mist
Pallidly rising when the summer droughts are done.

I have seen the lightning-blade, the leaping star,
    The caldrons of the sea in storm,
    Have felt the earthquake's lifting arm,
And trodden where abysmal fires and snowcones are.

I learn to prophesy the hid eclipse,
    The coming of eccentric orbs;
    To mete the dust the sky absorbs,
To weigh the sun, and fix the hour each planet dips.

I witness fellow earth-men surge and strive;
    Assemblies meet, and throb, and part;
    Death's soothing finger, sorrow's smart;
—All the vast various moils that mean a world alive.

But that I fain would wot of shuns my sense—
    Those sights of which old prophets tell,
    Those signs the general word so well,
Vouchsafed to their unheed, denied my watchings tense.

In graveyard green, behind his monument
    To glimpse a phantom parent, friend,
    Wearing his smile, and "Not the end!"
Outbreathing softly: that were blest enlightenment;

Or, if a dead Love's lips, whom dreams reveal
    When midnight imps of King Decay
    Delve sly to solve me back to clay,
Should leave some print to prove her spirit-kisses real;

Or, when Earth's Frail lie bleeding of her Strong,
      If some Recorder, as in Writ,
      Near to the weary scene should flit
And drop one plume as pledge that Heaven inscrolls the
      wrong.

—There are who, rapt to heights of trancéd trust,
      These tokens claim to feel and see,
      Read radiant hints of times to be—
Of heart to heart returning after dust to dust.

Such scope is granted not my powers indign...
      I have lain in dead men's beds, have walked
      The tombs of those with whom I'd talked,
Called many a gone and goodly one to shape a sign,

And panted for response. But none replies;
      No warnings loom, nor whisperings
      To open out my limitings,
And Nescience mutely muses: When a man falls he lies.

The Shadow on the Stone

I went by the Druid stone
  That broods in the garden white and lone,
And I stopped and looked at the shifting shadows
  That at some moments fall thereon
  From the tree hard by with a rhythmic swing,
  And they shaped in my imagining
To the shade that a well-known head and shoulders
  Threw there when she was gardening.

I thought her behind my back,
  Yea, her I long had learned to lack,
And I said: 'I am sure you are standing behind me,
  Though how do you get into this old track?'
  And there was no sound but the fall of a leaf
  As a sad response; and to keep down grief
I would not turn my head to discover
  That there was nothing in my belief.

    Yet I wanted to look and see
      That nobody stood at the back of me;
But I thought once more: 'Nay, I'll not unvision
    A shape which, somehow, there may be.'
    So I went on softly from the glade,
      And left her behind me throwing her shade,
As she were indeed an apparition—
    My head unturned lest my dream should fade.

Oscar Wilde
(1854–1900)

Requiescat

Tread lightly, she is near
  Under the snow,
Speak gently, she can hear
  The daisies grow.

All her bright golden hair
  Tarnished with rust,
She that was young and fair
  Fallen to dust.

Lily-like, white as snow,
  She hardly knew
She was a woman, so
  Sweetly she grew.

Coffin-board, heavy stone,
  Lie on her breast,
I vex my heart alone
  She is at rest.

Peace, Peace, she cannot hear
  Lyre or sonnet,
All my life's buried here,
  Heap earth upon it.

W. B. Yeats
(1865–1939)

He Wishes his Beloved were Dead

Were you but lying cold and dead,
And lights were paling out of the West,
You would come hither, and bend your head,
And I would lay my head on your breast;
And you would murmur tender words,
Forgiving me, because you were dead:
Nor would you rise and hasten away,
Though you have the will of wild birds,
But know your hair was bound and wound
About the stars and moon and sun:
O would, beloved, that you lay
Under the dock-leaves in the ground,
While lights were paling one by one.

Bibliography

'A Farewell to False Love.' First published in *Psalmes, Sonnets and Songs*, 1588.

'Sonnet 3'. First published in *Shakespeares Sonnets. Neuer before imprinted*, 1609.

'Sonnet 4'. First published in *Shakespeares Sonnets. Neuer before imprinted*, 1609.

'The Sick Rose'. Composed sometime after 1789. First published in *Songs of Innocence and of Experience*, 1794.

'The Mermaid'. First published in *Poems*, 1800.

'Basil'. First published in *Tales of Superstition and Chivalry*, 1802.

'Kubla Khan'. Completed in 1797. First published in *Christabel; Kubla Khan, A Vision; The Pains of Sleep*, 1816.

'Christabel'. First published in *Christabel; Kubla Khan, A Vision; The Pains of Sleep*, 1816.

'And Thou Art Dead, as Young and Fair'. First published in *Childe Harold*, 1812.

'When We Two Parted'. Written in 1808. First published in *Poems*, 1816.

'The Cold Earth Slept Below'. Published posthumously in *Hunt's Literary Pocket-Book*, 1823.

'An Invite, to Eternity'. Written in 1848. First published in *The Literary World*, September 1893.

'La Belle Dame Sans Merci'. Written in 1819. First published in the *Indicator*, May 1820.

'Bright Star, Would I Were Stedfast as Thou Art'. First published posthumously in *The Plymouth and Devonport Weekly Journal*, 1838.

'Sonnet 28'. First published in *Sonnets from the Portuguese*, 1850.

'Sonnet 43'. First published in *Sonnets from the Portuguese*, 1850.

'Lenore'. First published in *The Pioneer*, February, 1843. An earlier version appeared in 1831 under the title *A Pæan*.

'The Haunted Palace'. First published in *American Museum*, April 1839.

'The Raven'. First published in *New York Evening Mirror*, 29th January 1845.

'A Dream Within a Dream'. First published in *The Flag of Our Union*, March 1849.

'Annabel Lee'. First published on 9th October 1849 in the *New-York Daily Tribune*.

'The Lady of Shalott'. First published in *Poems, 1832* (incorrectly dated 1833) and another version published in *Poems, 1842*.

'Spellbound'. Written in 1837.

'Remembrance'. Written in 1845. First published in *Poems by Currer, Ellis, and Acton Bell*, 1846.

'A Carcass'. First published originally in French in 1857. Translated into English by Richard Herne Shepherd, *Translations from Charles Baudelaire*, 1869.

'The Ghost'. First published originally in French in 1857. Translated into English by F. P. Sturm, *Baudelaire: His Prose and Poetry*, 1919.

'The Death of Lovers'. First published originally in French in 1857. Translated into English by F. P. Sturm, *Baudelaire: His Prose and Poetry*, 1919.

'After Death'. Written in April, 1849. First published in *Goblin Market and Other Poems*, 1862.

'Echo'. Written in 1854. First published in *Goblin Market and Other Poems*, 1862.

'Song'. Written in 1848. First published in *Goblin Market and Other Poems*, 1862.

'Jessie Cameron'. First published in *The Prince's Progress and Other Poems*, 1866.

'A Sign-Seeker'. First published in *Wessex Poems and Other Verses*, 1898.

'The Shadow on the Stone'. First published in
Moments of Vision and Miscellaneous Verses, 1917.

'Requiescat'. Written in 1874. First published in
Poems, 1881.

'He Wishes His Beloved Were Dead'. First published
in the *Sketch*, 1898 under the title *Aodh to Decotra*.

Made in the USA
Middletown, DE
03 June 2024

55239648R00087